Storage solutions

in a weekend

Storage solutions

in a weekend

Julie London

MEREHURST

Acknowledgements

Thanks to everyone who has worked on this book – a testament to team effort.

Reprinted 1998
First published 1997 by Merehurst Limited,
Ferry House, 51–57 Lacy Road, London, SW15 1PR

ISBN 1-85391-796-6

A catalogue record for this book is available from the British Library.

Editor: Geraldine Christy
Designer: Anthony Cohen
Photographer: Lucinda Symons
Stylist: Denise Brock

Colour separation by Bright Arts, Hong Kong
Printed in Singapore by Tien Wah Press

Contents

Introduction

Welcome to the world of weekend storage. One thing is for sure – if I can make these projects, then so can you! I am a great believer in 'having a go', and you must be too, otherwise you probably would not be reading this book.

All of these projects are easily attainable in a weekend. Some will take longer than others; the ottoman and Formica wardrobe makeover will probably take the most time, as both projects involve a fair amount of work. The larger projects will need two people to complete them, but the smaller ones are easily handled by one person, although it may be useful to have a helper on hand.

I have tried very hard to make each project relevant to today's small-home lifestyle, where space and money are in short supply, and where rooms have to be used for several different purposes. The projects have been chosen to solve specific storage problems, but many of them can be used for a number of applications. For instance, the wire bathroom shelf can also be used for holding letters on a hallway wall. The wall ladder could be hung from the ceiling, or used to hold the ironing. The ottoman can also double up as extra seating, and the folding screen can hide piles of clutter, or simply act as a room divider.

The projects have also been designed to use simple materials that are readily available. You will find that most DIY stores will cut wood to size for you, providing you are buying it from them, of course. Some stores may charge a token fee, but most will give you the first two cuts free. Anyway, it is worth a small charge to be able to fit the wood into your car and it saves the trouble of having to cut it to the right size yourself.

All the tools I have used can be bought from large DIY stores, with the exception of the round-nosed pliers for the bathroom shelf project. You will need to buy the pliers from a specialist tool supplier – look these up in *Yellow Pages* or a similar trade directory. You may already have some of the necessary tools, or be able to borrow them from friends or family.

A brief word about safety! Always take care when using electrical equipment – use a circuit breaker, which cuts off the electrical supply if you accidentally slice through a wire. Unplug appliances when you are not using them, and always put them away safely after use.

When cutting MDF always wear a mask. MDF is made up of particles of wood and dust and degenerates into this when it is cut, especially with a jigsaw. A mask will help to prevent you breathing in the dust particles.

An important point to remember is that if things go wrong when you are working on a project or if they do not turn out exactly as expected, there is always something to be salvaged from the situation. Mistakes add charm and character; a little quirkiness goes a long way and at least you know your storage really will be unique.

Making the projects may not necessarily be cheap, but it will definitely be a lot less expensive than buying the equivalent ready made. Besides, you cannot beat the satisfaction of making something from nothing and, as in the case of the wardrobe makeover, perhaps transforming something that is reviled into a stylish and useful piece of furniture. The discipline of making something yourself is very fulfilling and when the finished piece is admired by your friends and family you will have an immense feeling of pride.

When I started writing this book I was in dire need of some storage solutions myself. Now many of the projects are displayed proudly in my own home. I look at the wire bathroom shelf every day, filled with bright glass bottles that catch the morning light, I can hide my ironing behind a folding screen and the CD tower now contains about a quarter of my music collection – I must make some more towers! In fact, most of the projects evolved as a means to solve the problem of my own clutter.

I hope that this book will be a starting point for you, and that you will not only make and adapt these projects, but also develop your own storage ideas.

Have a good weekend!

Julie London

Curtain-covered alcove

Reminiscent of simply furnished seaside holiday homes, this is a modern and smart interpretation of a makeshift wardrobe. It is ideal for storing all types of clutter.

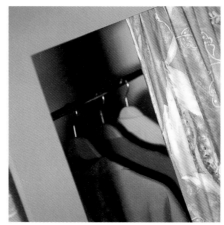

Alcoves almost cry out to be shelved or made into wardrobes of some sort. Here, colour turns the alcove into a focal point – bright vermilion and purple are an unusual combination and make the most of a simple idea.

Each curtain is made from only one 137 cm (54 in) width of fabric, so it is an economical treatment – you could even use a large remnant. Behind these curtains is a clothes rail, but this idea could equally be used to hide a small office, or a freestanding hanging rail. There is plenty of room for a complete storage system with baskets, rails and shoe racks. If your alcove is deep enough, the curtains could even disguise a computer workstation or several unsightly filing cabinets.

The high top shelf is useful for boxes and seasonal sports gear, but you could add further shelving for storing smaller items. You might decide to curtain in the top layer as well. In this case simply follow the same steps for the battens, facing and curtains, making sure you measure the required lengths carefully.

The curtain track is on the inside of the front edge, so the heading tape has to be sewn onto the right side of the fabric.

Planning your time

DAY ONE
AM: Measure alcove and buy materials. Fix battens to inside edges of alcove. Screw hanging rail to walls.

PM: Make MDF top shelf. Fix softwood face onto battens. Attach curtain track. Join centre piece. Prime.

DAY TWO
AM: Apply top coat. Make curtains.

PM: Apply second coat. Hang curtains.

Tools and materials

25 x 33 mm (1 x 1¼ in) softwood for battens

15 mm (½ in) MDF for shelf

100 x 20 mm (4 x ¾ in) softwood for facing

Spirit level

Hanging rail

Curtain track

2 mending plates

Offcut of softwood to support centre piece

Primer paint

Eggshell topcoat paint

Fabric for curtains

Heading tape

Curtain hooks

Sewing machine

Jigsaw

Day One

Step 1

First make the top shelf. Cut a sheet of MDF to the width of the alcove but not quite as deep. Fix softwood batten supports on the back and side walls of the alcove. Use a spirit level to get them all straight.

Step 2

Screw softwood battens at right angles to the shelf on both sides of the alcove. You will need to drill pilot holes through the wood and into the plaster. Enlarge both holes and insert wall plugs to hold the screws. Use a spirit level to make sure the battens are straight.

Step 3

The hanging rail needs to be in the centre of the sides of the alcove, measuring front to back. Mark the centre point and decide how high you want the rail to be; 165 cm (65 in) from the floor is a good height for dresses and long coats. Again, use a spirit level to make sure the rail is straight.

1

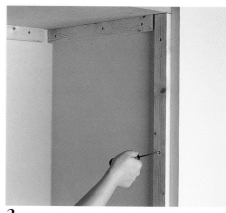

2

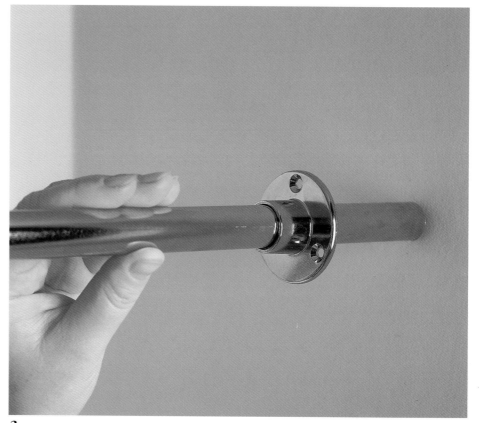

3

Using a spirit level

Make sure lines are straight with a spirit level. Hold it along the top of whatever it is you need to be straight and adjust it until the air bubble is in the middle. A spirit level enables you to check both horizontal and vertical directions.

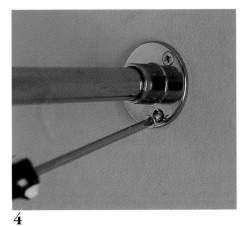

4

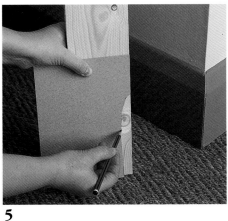

5

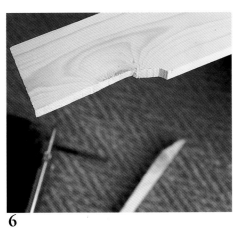

6

7

8

Step 4

Secure the hanging rail in place by screwing the fixing plate to the alcove wall at each end.

Step 5

For the outside edges of the alcove, cut two 170 cm (68 in) pieces of 100 x 20 mm (4 x ¾ in) softwood to allow for the width of the facing. Cut out a card template of the profile of the skirting and transfer the outline to the bottom of both pieces of softwood, reversing the pattern for one of them.

Step 6

Secure the softwood in a vice and cut following the skirting outline using a jigsaw.

Step 7

Nail the side pieces onto the battening.

Step 8

Cut another piece of 100 x 20 mm (4 x ¾ in) softwood to the width of the alcove. Fix a curtain track along its length, 5 cm (2 in) from the inside lower edge.

Step 9

Nail the top piece of the facing onto the side battens and shelf. It should sit just above the MDF shelf.

Step 10

To make the central piece, attach a 100 x 20 mm (4 x ¾ in) piece of softwood, cut to size, to the middle of the top piece from inside the alcove. Use joining plates, making a large 'T' (Although this join will be inside the alcove, it has been photographed separately here to provide a clear view of the technique).

Step 11

To support the bottom of the central piece, nail a block of wood behind it, to the floor, making sure the piece is straight with a spirit level. Nail the central piece to the block of wood. Prime all the wood and leave to dry thoroughly overnight.

9

10

11

Priming wood

All bare or new wood should be primed before painting. Use an all-purpose primer or special wood primer. If you are using a wood like pine, which has lots of knots, it should be treated with knotting to stop the natural resins bleeding through the finished paintwork.

12

Day Two

Step 12

Apply the top coat colour, and while the paint is drying, make two curtains, one for each side of the alcove. Measure the width by the height of each aperture. You should be able to get away with one width of fabric per curtain. Hem the sides, top and bottom edges on the wrong side.

Step 13

Turn the curtains over and pin the heading tape onto the right sides of the fabric.

Step 14

Machine the heading tape in place. Gather the tops of the curtains to fit the alcove and insert hooks to correspond with the track. Apply the second coat of paint to the wood, and, when dry, hang the curtains.

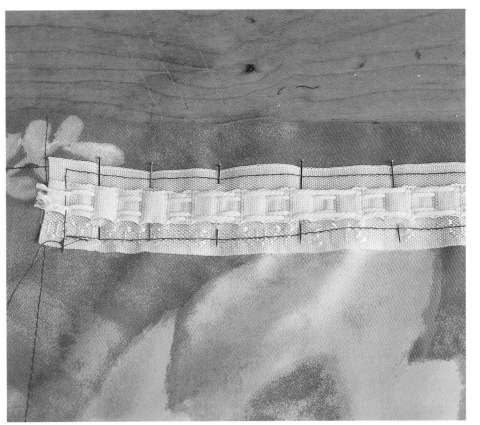

13

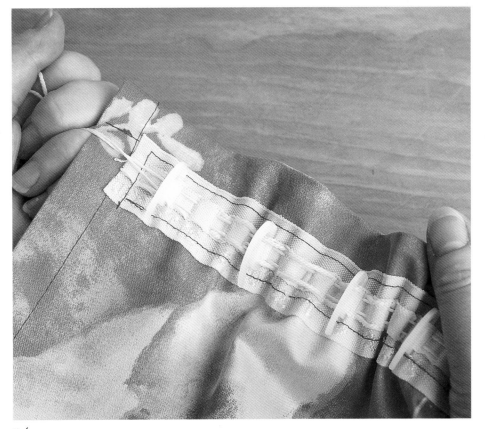

14

Wire bathroom shelf

Bright bottles and soaps add a sophisticated finishing touch to a bathroom, and a hand-made shelf like this is ideal to hold them all. A pattern of hearts has universal appeal.

Planning your time

DAY ONE
AM: Twist wire. Make the back heart.

PM: Make the front and side supports. Make the back two, smaller hearts.

DAY TWO
AM: Twist more wire if necessary. Make the small single hearts.

PM: Bind the small hearts to the sides.

Tools and materials

Galvanized wire (3 lengths of 3 m [10 ft] are needed; each will make 1.5 m [5 ft] when twisted, giving you 4.5 m [15 ft] altogether)

Soft florists' wire

Round-nosed pliers

Wire-cutters or good quality combination pliers

The shelf should only really take you a day to make, but it is hard work on the fingers so you might want to take two days over it. You may also need someone to hold onto one end of the wire around an offcut of wood, while you twist; failing that, use the method demonstrated in the steps.

Twist more wire than you think you will need as there will be some wastage, but, when twisting extra lengths, try to ensure that the tension is the same, so that the effect of the whole piece will be consistent.

Start the shelf by making the back so that you get the overall size right, but you can make it to suit whatever you intend to put in it. Once the wire is bound together it is quite strong and should be able to take reasonably heavy items, but be careful not to overload it.

A shelf like this can be used in various other rooms in the home. You might find one useful in the kitchen for holding cooking utensils or pot scourers and cloths. You could also use one as a handy letter rack in the hall, or for holding stationery items in a home office.

Once you have made a shelf, you can make all sorts of other things using twisted wire – small items such as soapdishes or toothbrush holders might be fun to make. Try planning your own designs as well as heart shapes.

1

Day One

Step 1

Twist several lengths of wire around a door handle – about 1.5 m (5 ft) at a time is manageable. To do this cut 3 m (10 ft) of wire. Bend it in half, then put the doubled end around a door knob. Twisting the wire is quite tricky to do as it has a tendency to spring off the handle if you do not hold it taut. Wind the other two ends around a piece of wood, pull the wire tight and twist anti-clockwise until all the wire is twisted and starts to buckle. Release the tension, but do not let go of the wood; just let the wire untwist itself slightly. Cut the wire off the door handle and piece of wood.

Step 2

To make the back, centre heart, take a piece of the twisted wire and bend it, gently, in two, crossing one piece over the other as shown in the photograph.

Step 3

Using florists' wire, bind the point where the twisted wire crosses, so that it does not move about.

2

3

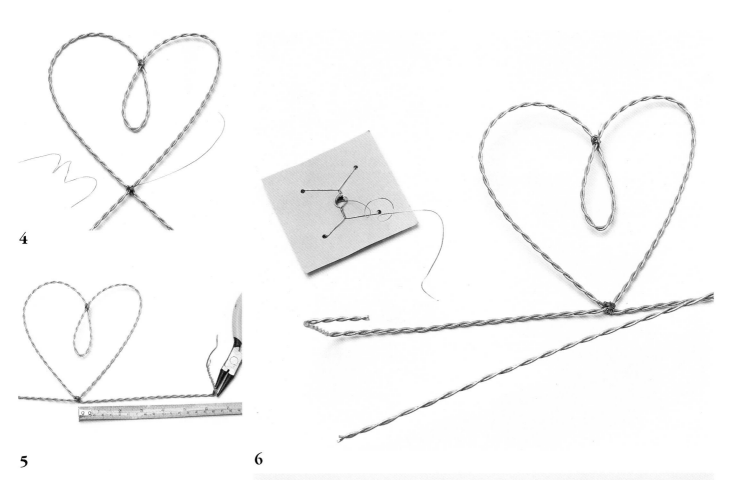

4

5

6

Step 4

Bend the wire round beyond the bound, crossed point and down into a heart shape and bind it at the point of the heart. Do not worry too much about making the heart a regular shape.

Step 5

Straighten the back, with round-nosed pliers. Next, measuring 17 cm (6¾ in) from the point of the heart, bend the wire to make a right angle. Measure 7 cm (2¾ in) and bend another right angle. Repeat this process on the other side of the heart.

Step 6

Cut a 34 cm (13½ in) length of wire and bind it onto the front of the frame.

Step 7

Bind both sides. Then cut two 50 cm (20 in) lengths of wire. With round-nosed pliers, bend right angles on both pieces, 8 cm (3 in) from each end. Bind to front and back of the main frame.

7

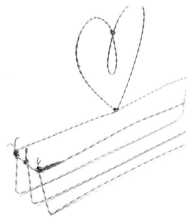

8

Step 8

Cut another 50 cm (20 in) length of wire, bend it as in Step 7 and bind it into the centre of the frame.

Step 9

With round-nosed pliers, separate the ends of excess wire protruding above the top edge of the frame. Twist each single piece of wire away from the centre and around onto itself to make a little bow.

Step 10

To make the left-hand front support and back heart, cut a 60 cm (24 in) length of wire, bend a right angle and bind it to the front 10 cm (4 in) from the left side.

9

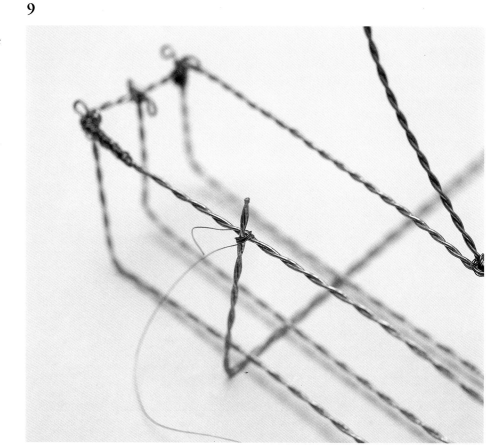

10

11

Step 11

Bind the wire to the main frame as shown in the photograph and bend it into another right angle, up the back of the frame. Repeat Step 10 with another 60 cm (24 in) length of wire on the right-hand side.

Step 12

Where the hearts join the back, bend the wire to the right (or left depending on which heart you are making) and pull it round into a smaller version of the centre one. Secure it with florists' wire and snip off any excess. Repeat with the other heart, then bind them all together with wire.

Day Two

Step 13

Make smaller hearts from single pieces of wire to fit on the front and sides, again binding them onto the frame with florists' wire.

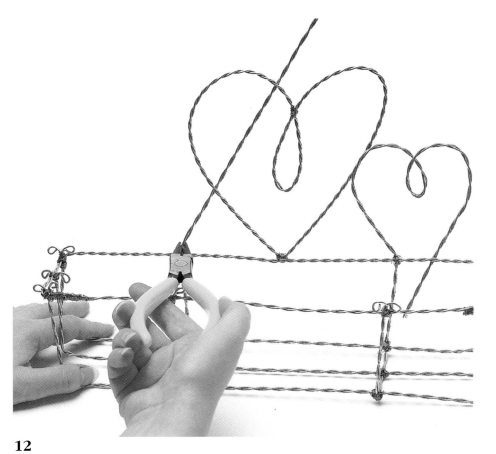

12

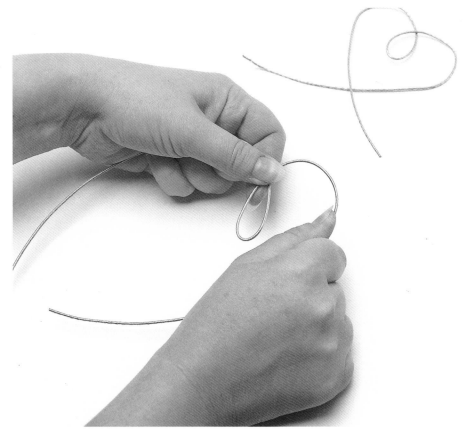

13

Wall ladder

This fun idea can be put to use wherever you need extra storage. The ladder is not meant to be a permanent fixture, so is suitable for any room in the house.

Planning your time

DAY ONE
AM: Buy your materials, cut uprights to length and mark position of rungs. Drill the holes.

PM: Cut rungs to size, whittle the ends to fit in the holes; glue in place.

DAY TWO
AM: Shape the ends of the uprights; paint the ladder.

PM: Sand the ladder to age it.

Tools and materials

37 mm (1½ in) dowel
29 mm (1¼ in) dowel
20 mm (¾ in) flat wood drill bit
Stanley knife
String
PVA glue
Paint
Sandpaper
Vice
Masking tape

The idea for this 'store and display' piece came from a Provençal-style kitchen; it evokes the image of bunches of herbs and battered pots and pans hanging from a rustic ladder. Something like this is ideal if you are living in a rented home and do not want to spend money on items that you cannot take away with you.

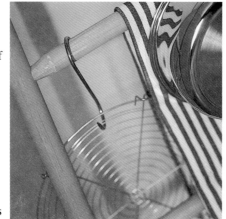

If you have the space the ladder could be hung from the ceiling with chains, or suspended on chunky pieces of rope. This idea would transfer quite readily to a bathroom, where you can hang toiletries in bags or baskets; or to a utility room, where the ironing could be hung over the rungs.

You could also use the ladder as portable hanging space for guests' clothes in a spare room. Versions in a variety of sizes might look fun arranged in order of height.

The ladder shown here is painted, but it would look equally attractive with the grain of the wood showing – simply varnish it to protect the surface. It could also be stained – a wide range of colours is available as well as natural wood shades.

Although the ladder is sturdy and can support quite weighty pots and pans, it is not strong enough to climb on, so do not be tempted!

Day One

Step 1

Cut two 185 cm (6 ft) lengths of 37 mm (1½ in) dowel for the sides of the ladder. To work out the positions for the rungs, I started the first rung 45 cm (17¾ in) from the bottom and then every 30 cm (12 in). The top rung is 15 cm (6 in) from the top. These measurements do not have to be completely accurate, they just need to look right.

Lay the dowels on the floor and hold them in place with masking tape so that you can mark out the measurements easily.

Step 2

Hold the dowel in a vice and drill halfway through its thickness with a 20 mm (¾ in) flat wood drill bit. Mark the depth on the drill bit and drill the other holes, using this as a depth gauge.

Lay both dowels on the ground to decide how wide you want the rungs to be. I inclined the dowels so that the top was narrower than the bottom, but you can make the ladder straight if you wish. The rungs are cut from 29 mm (1¼ in) dowel. Measure the width of each rung and add 2 cm (¾ in) for the ends that will be glued into the holes. Hold the rung dowel firmly, preferably in a vice, and cut with a saw or jigsaw.

Step 3

To ensure the rungs fit in the holes, mark a circle 20 mm (¾ in) in diameter on the ends of each rung.

Step 4

Using a Stanley knife, start shaving the rungs down to the marked circles roughly 2 cm (¾ in) from each end until they fit in the holes.

Step 5

Glue the rungs into the main frame. Put plenty of glue in the holes and push the rungs in as far as they will go.

1

2

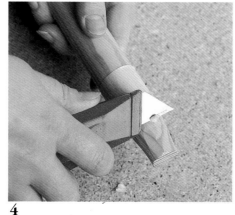

3

4

5

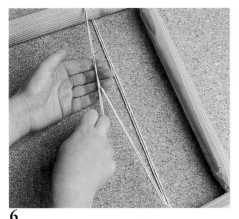

6

7

8

Step 6

Tie string around the top, bottom and middle of the ladder to keep the pieces in place while the glue is drying.

Step 7

Tighten the string by twisting it with an offcut of wood or a spoon. This ensures the rungs are as tight in their holes as possible. Leave to dry overnight.

Day Two

Step 8

When the glue is completely dry and the ladder is stable, shave a little off the ends of the uprights and sand them smooth to make rounded ends.

Step 9

Apply a coat of emulsion paint, using a dry brush and very little paint as shown in Step 10. Do not hide the grain completely, but brush the paint out.

Step 10

Use only a little paint at a time on your brush, and wipe off any excess onto a piece of newspaper.

Step 11

When the paint is completely dry (usually after four hours or so), lightly rub away some of the paint. Do this particularly on the joints of the rungs, to make the ladder look as if it has worn with age.

9

10

11

Transforming a Formica wardrobe

You can never have too much storage, even if you hate the sight of the furniture. Here is an idea for transforming an unattractive wardrobe into a stunning showpiece.

Nearly all of us have furniture that we do not like but cannot afford to replace just yet. But with a coat of paint and a jigsaw you can transform your ordinary furniture – not quite into family heirlooms, but at least into something of which you can be proud.

Who would believe this is the same wardrobe as shown in the 'before' photograph below? I bought this wardrobe very cheaply from a local charity shop and and have transformed it into an armoire by adding some chicken wire, paint and new handles.

When painting Formica, or any other shiny surface, you need to 'key' the surface well, so that the paint will adhere properly. Thoroughly rub down the furniture with wire wool, then paint on a coat of primer or tile primer followed by undercoat before painting on the top colour.

The pediment and base board were shaped from offcuts of pine used for other projects, as they were the same thickness as the doors. I used a jigsaw to cut out the hand-drawn design. Shop-bought legs replaced the castors. The dramatic fabric chosen here gives the finished wardrobe a bold impact, but with a more subtle pattern it could be turned into a country-style piece. You could also try experimenting with different shapes for the pediment and base board.

The junk shop wardrobe before it was transformed into a thoroughly stylish storage solution

1

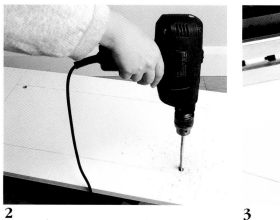

2

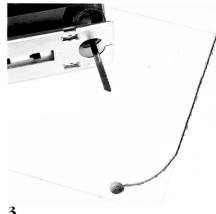

3

Day One

Step 1

Take the doors off the wardrobe, lay them on the floor and measure out the positions of the panels, using a piece of batten as a guide to help you draw the lines straight.

Step 2

Drill two pilot holes on the opposite diagonal corners of each panel to be cut. I drilled my holes in the top right-hand and bottom left-hand corners. Use a small drill bit so as not to split the wood and enlarge the holes using a flat wood drill bit. The holes need to be big enough to get a jigsaw blade into.

Step 3

Starting in one corner, cut the top line of the panel up to the opposite corner, as shown in the photograph. Remove the jigsaw.

Step 4

Turn the jigsaw around and put the blade back into the cut, so that it is heading the opposite way to the first cut. Cut up to the corner. Remove the jigsaw.

4

Using a mitre box

Cutting a mitre is a lot easier with a mitre block. Lay the piece of wood in the mitre block and hold it tight against one side. Place the tenon saw in the two corresponding slots on either side of the mitre block and draw it backwards and forwards until the wood is cut. Mitre blocks will cut both left- and right-hand mitres.

5

6

7

Step 5
Put the jigsaw back into the pilot hole and cut down the right-hand side of the panel, to the bottom corner. Turn the jigsaw round and cut back up to the top corner. Continue this method of cutting to complete the panel, then cut the other panels like this.

Step 6
Rub the doors and carcass of the wardrobe with wire wool to make a key for the primer paint to adhere to.

Step 7
Mitre one end of the right-angled beading.

Step 8
Measure the beading against the inside of the cut panels and cut to fit. Do this on all the pieces of beading so they fit inside the cut panels.

8

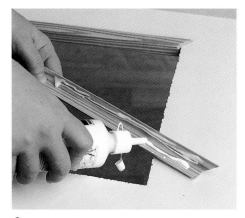

9

10

11

Step 9
Glue all the mitred beading onto the inside of the cut panels. You might need to double check that the pieces fit before you glue them in place.

Step 10
Secure the beading with panel pins.

Step 11
Fill any gaps in the joins with filler and sand down. Prime the doors, beading and carcass of the wardrobe.

Day Two

Step 12
Paint the front of the doors and the carcass with the first coat of colour. Cut the chicken wire into panels with wire cutters to fit behind each door panel. Be careful when cutting the wire, as it is easy to scratch yourself.

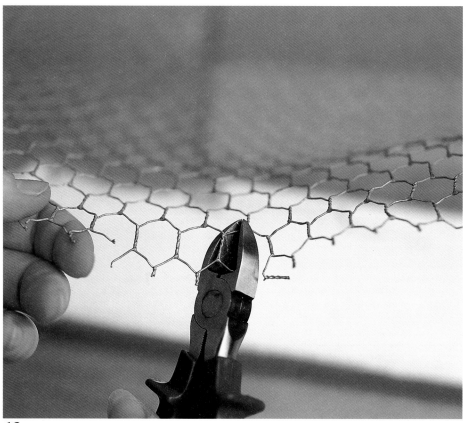

12

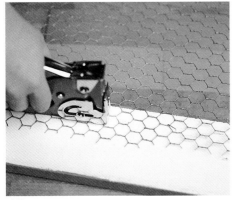

13

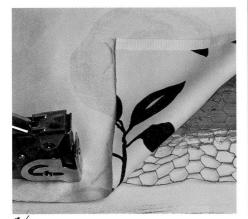

14

15

Step 13
Staple the wire panels on the reverse side of the doors and cut off any excess.

Step 14
Cut the fabric to fit, making sure the pattern fits into each panel. Staple the pieces to the back of the door. Trim the fabric so that the doors close easily.

Step 15
Remove the castors, make pilot holes for screws and screw on leg plates.

Step 16
Replace the bottom plinth with a piece of shaped wood. Cut a piece of pine to the same length, draw your pattern along the bottom edge and cut it out, then sand and prime it. Screw it, from underneath, to the bottom of the wardrobe. Make a shaped pediment for the top, then sand and prime it. Screw in the legs. Apply two or three coats of top colour paint to the whole wardrobe and fix on new handles.

16

Hanging shelves on chains

Chains are a different, stylish way to support shelves. Although mostly suitable for lighter objects, they provide additional storage as well as an interesting display.

Before you begin this project you need to tap your ceiling to ascertain the position of your ceiling joists. There will be a more dense sound when you tap the joist. Gravity will ensure that the chains hang straight; therefore the hooks need to be positioned in line with the joists.

Work out the length of chains you need before you go to buy them, and get them cut by the hardware shop – you will never be able to cut them yourself unless you have a pair of bolt clippers. If you have concrete floors, wing bolts will secure the chain to them. These bolts expand as they are tightened and therefore grip the concrete. With wooden floors you can use large hooks screwed into the floor.

These shelves on chains have clean, modern lines and are best suited to a room where they can be used as storage for items that are used occasionally rather than constantly. They add an attractive dimension to a home office or study. As well as being functional, their light, airy feel will help make the task of book-keeping or filing, or even homework, less irksome.

Planning your time

DAY ONE
AM: Buy your materials. Work out the lengths of the chains and get them cut in the hardware shop. Screw hooks into the joists.

PM: Colourwash the shelves. Attach screw eyes to the corners.

DAY TWO
AM: Hang the chains and shelves. Drill holes in the floor and screw in wing bolts. Tension the shelves.

PM: Arrange items on shelves.

Tools and materials

4 heavy-duty screws with long threads

16 screw eyes

16 'S' hooks

2 planed pine surfaces to fit the alcove

Enough chain to reach from ceiling to floor (4 times this length)

4 wing bolts with hook heads (for concrete floor) or 4 heavy-duty screws as for the ceiling

12 mm (½ in) drill bit (for concrete floor)

Paint

Day One

Step 1

Measure and cut the boards to the correct size, then position where you want the screw eyes to be, measuring from the edge of the shelf. Measure the distance from the wall that you want the shelves to hang, drill a small pilot hole into the ceiling joist and screw in the first hook. Drill another pilot hole in front of the first for the second hook. It should be less than the depth of the shelf.

Repeat for the other side.

Step 2

Colourwash both sides and edges of the pine boards with watered-down emulsion paint – use one part paint to four parts water. Leave to dry.

Step 3

When the paint is dry, put the boards together and drill small pilot holes 3 cm (1¼ in) in from each corner, going right through the first board to mark the second.

Step 4

Enlarge the pilot holes on the first board to accommodate the thickness of the screws. Take care not to drill right through to the other side.

Step 5

Screw the eye screws in the top board. Use a screwdriver as a lever to turn the screws. Make sure the thread does not go right through the board and come out the other side. Do the same on the second board, but insert the eye screws to the underside rather than the top.

1

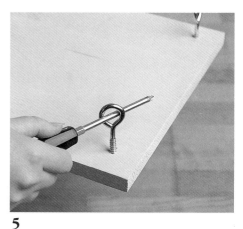

2

3

4

5

6

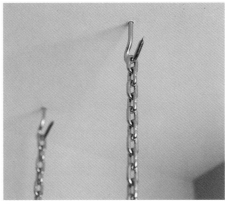

7

8

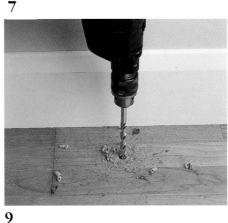

9

10

Step 6

Turn the shelves over and mark the position of the screws, 1 cm (½ in) nearer the edge than the first ones. These screws will be on the underside of the top shelf and the top side of the bottom shelf. Again, drill pilot holes and screw in the hooks as described in Step 5. The photograph shows clearly how they should look.

Day Two

Step 7

Hang chains from the ceiling hooks.

Step 8

Hang 'S' hooks from the ends of the chains and hang the top shelf from these. Hang 'S' hooks from the underside of the top shelf, then chains, then 'S' hooks, then the bottom shelf. Hang 'S' hooks and chains from the underside of the bottom shelf and wing bolts from these. Make a mark on the floor where the wing bolts hang.

Step 9

Remove the chains from the underside of the bottom shelf and drill pilot holes in the floor for the positions of the wing bolts. Drill the bolt holes using a 12 mm (½ in) masonry drill bit.

Step 10

Screw the wing bolts into the floor. They will open out to grip the concrete or wood. Replace the chains on the underside of the last shelf and hang 'S' hooks to hook up with the wing bolts. This should hold the chains tight enough to stop them swaying around, but allow a little movement.

Peg rail

Peg rails are popular because of their versatility. Inspired by Shaker style, here is a simple peg rail that will provide storage for items that need to be close at hand.

The nineteenth-century American Shakers used peg rails to keep furniture and clutter off the floor so that there was more space to pray. They have become popular again due to the general interest in the simplicity of Shaker-style furnishings.

This peg rail is made from basic materials that are available at all DIY outlets and is not as complicated to make as it may seem. The back is made from pine, the pegs from dowelling and the trim from half-round beading. The only difficult part might be in getting all the pegs to stand the same way, so you may need to wiggle them around to get them right.

I used a water-based paint from a range of reproduction colours, which needed buffing with wire wool to work it into the grain of the wood. You could just as easily use a vinyl emulsion paint for use on walls – it would gradually wear – or an eggshell finish.

The peg rail can be made to any length – you could even fit it around an entire room, as the Shakers used to. It will look good in a bathroom for towels and toiletries; in a child's room with drawstring bags or baskets hanging from it for storing toys; in a kitchen, as here; or in a hallway for coats and hats. Fixed to the wall properly, it is also strong enough to hold lightweight folding chairs.

Planning your time

DAY ONE
AM: Buy your materials; cut rail and dowels to length.

PM: Mark the position of the pegs, drill holes and hammer in pegs. Make grooves in pegs and glue on beading.

DAY TWO
AM: Apply paint and rub down with wire wool.

PM: Fix to the wall.

Tools and materials

100 x 20 mm (4 x ¾ in) softwood

20 mm (¾ in) dowel

20 mm (¾ in) flat wood drill bit

Junior hacksaw

Stanley knife

Hammer

Coarse sandpaper

12 mm (½ in) half-round beading

PVA glue

Wire wool

Paint

Day One

Step 1

Cut a piece of softwood (pine) to the length you want for the back of the rail or ask the timber merchant to do this for you. I had my piece of wood cut to 50 cm (19¾ in). To mark the centre of the back piece, and therefore the central position of the pegs, cut a piece of paper the same size as the peg rail. Fold it in half lengthways, and place the folded edge along the top of the rail. Mark the position of the pegs, the first one 5 cm (2 in) in from the edge and then every 10 cm (4 in), making the last one also 5 cm (2 in) from the edge.

Step 2

Use a flat wood bit on a hand drill to make the holes for the pegs. Drill halfway through, then turn the wood over and drill through the back of the hole to prevent the wood splitting.

Step 3

Cut five pegs 5 cm (2 in) long, plus the depth of the back, from a piece of 20 mm (¾ in) dowel using a junior hacksaw. You might need to shave one end of the pegs if they are larger than the holes. Use a craft knife or Stanley knife and keep trying each peg in its hole until it fits snugly, but be careful not to shave off too much.

Step 4

Place each peg in its hole. Then, using a spare piece of wood to protect the pegs, hammer each one in separately. Make sure they are as straight as possible in the board.

Step 5

Make grooves across each peg by folding up a piece of coarse sandpaper and rubbing it across each peg in turn until you have made a shallow indentation. The grooves will prevent anything you hang on them falling off.

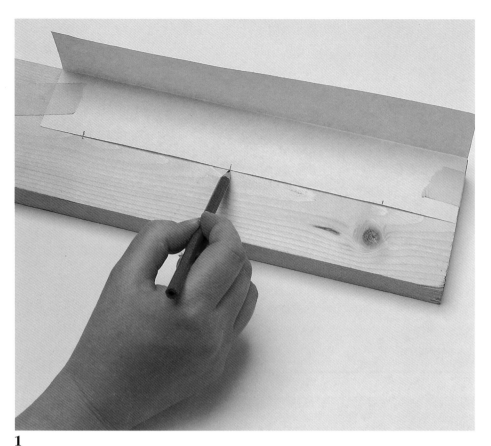

1

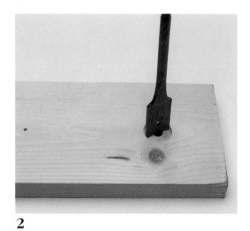

4

3

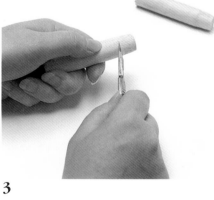

5

2

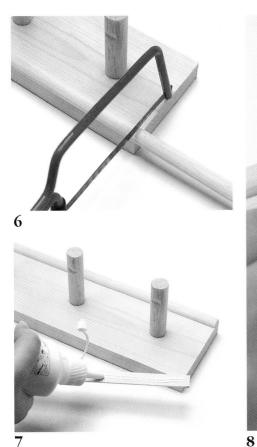

6

7

8

Step 6

Cut two pieces of beading, measuring them against the length of the back piece, and cut with a junior hacksaw.

Step 7

Glue the beading on each edge of the rail with PVA glue. Hold it in place until it is tacky and wipe off any excess glue.

Day Two

Step 8

I painted the peg rail with a specialist water-based paint, that needed buffing with wire wool to prevent the paint from gradually wearing off. You could use emulsion or eggshell.

Step 9

Buff up the peg rail with wire wool and use a sawing action to do the same to the pegs. If you have used an emulsion paint, apply two coats of varnish.

9

Ottoman

This ottoman is stylish enough in its own right to have on show, but it also provides you with storage space for magazines and brochures, and extra seating for unexpected guests.

Planning your time

DAY ONE

AM: Buy your materials. Construct the sides.

PM: Plane off the edges, make the base and lid.

DAY TWO

AM: Cover the lid with foam and fabric; screw together. Cover the box with fabric.

PM: Screw on the castors.

Tools and materials

Sheet of 15 mm (⅝ in) MDF, 1.2 x 2.4 m (4 x 8 ft)

Felt pen

Jigsaw with adjustable base plate

PVA glue

Drill

Countersinking tool (pilot hole drill bit)

Countersunk screws

Plane

Upholstery foam to fit the lid

Staple gun

Fabric to cover the box and lid

4 castors

The tapered sides of the ottoman give an air of elegance to an everyday piece of furniture, preventing it from looking too boxy. This is simple woodwork, using readily available materials, but you will need someone to help when you are joining the sides together.

First of all you need to work out the size of the ottoman on paper and draw a rough diagram of the pieces, with their measurements, as they would fit onto a sheet of 1.2 x 2.4 m (4 x 8 ft) MDF. Take the diagram with you when you buy the MDF and get it cut at the same time. Most DIY stores will cut it on site for you and it will be much easier to transport home in smaller pieces.

Foam has to be fire retardant and is available from upholsterers' suppliers. Do not be tempted to use old foam that you might have lying around, in case it is not safe. Staple the fabric in place so that it is easy to remove if you want to change it at a later date; a plaid fabric like this gives you an easy line to follow when matching up corners.

With castors fitted, the ottoman is easy to move around the room as required. You might also make a smaller version, perhaps to be used as a needlework box and as additional occasional seating. Look for suitable fabric remnants to keep the cost down.

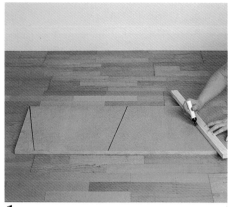

1

Day One

Step 1

Work out the size you want the ottoman to be. This will depend on the space available and what you want to put in it. The one shown here measures 90 cm (36 in) long x 40 cm (16 in) high x 45 cm (18 in) wide.

Cut a piece of MDF 42 x 90 cm (17 x 36 in); the two ends of the box can be cut from this one piece. Draw them side by side; one will be upside down (see photograph). The top of the end should be 53 cm (21 in) wide and the bottom of the end 32 cm (13 in). Draw the angles with a felt pen using a batten as a straightedge.

Step 2

Cut the box ends out with a jigsaw. Cut two side pieces of 40 cm (16 in) high x 90 cm (36 in) wide.

2

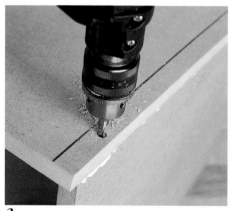

3

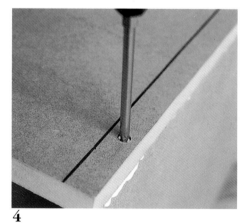

4

Step 3

Join the sides and ends together at right angles. The ends will sit proud of the sides as they are a little higher. Draw a line on each side of both ends to indicate the thickness of the MDF. Apply PVA glue to the sides. Using a countersink tool attachment for a hand drill, drill three holes along the length of the end of the box, so that they go through into the thickness of the sides.

Step 4

Fix the screws so that the heads are countersunk (ie. they lie below the surface of the wood).

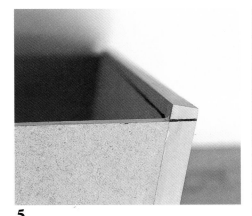

5

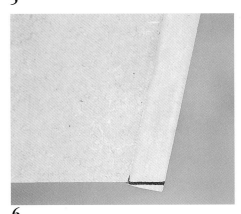

6

7

Step 5

Where the ends sit proud of the sides of the ottoman, draw a line on them front to back and along the inside and outside at the same height as the sides.

Step 6

Draw a line on the base where the ends sit proud of the sides.

Step 7

Set the blade on the jigsaw at an angle to line up with the angle on the edge of the box and cut off the excess. Repeat on the other side and the base. The angle on the jigsaw remains the same.

Step 8

Plane the edges smooth. Cut the base of the box to fit. Do this by placing the box on a piece of MDF and draw around the inside perimeter. Cut out the base with a jigsaw using the blade set at the same angle for cutting the long side edges, but set the blade straight for cutting the short ends.

8

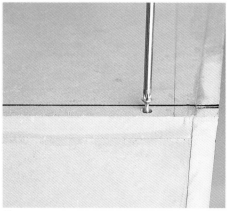

9

Step 9

Join the base to the frame in the same way that the sides and ends were joined. Countersink the screws using a pilot drill attachment.

Step 10

To make the lid, cut a piece of MDF the same size as the top. Cut a smaller piece to fit the inside of the lid, deducting 1 cm (½ in) all around for the thickness of the fabric. The long edges of the inside need to be angled for a snug fit, so use the jigsaw blade at the same angle as you used for trimming the box. The short edges are cut with the blade at a right angle.

Centre the inside piece of MDF on the lid and countersink three screw holes to attach the inside to the lid. Be careful not to let the drill holes go through to the top side of the lid.

Day Two

Step 11

Remove the inside of the lid and glue a piece of foam the same size to the top of the lid (you can get this cut to size by an upholsterer). Cover the lid with your chosen fabric, stapling the two ends first to get the fabric tight, then the sides. MDF is quite hard to work on so you may need to hit the staples home with a hammer.

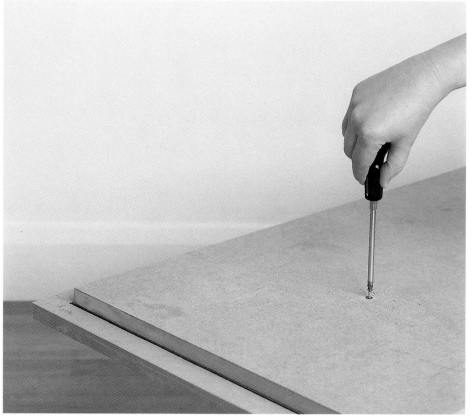

10

11

12

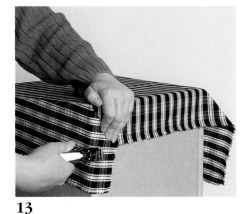

13

14

Step 12

Fold in the corners neatly and staple them. Replace the inside of the lid and screw it in place.

Step 13

Next, cover the ends of the box. Turn the box on one end and work as shown in the photograph.

Step 14

Tuck the ends over into the inside, folding the corners neatly and stapling the fabric in place.

Step 15

To cover the sides, measure the width of the ottoman and press under a small hem on the edge of the fabric. Staple the fabric along the edges of the ottoman, under the base and up over the top, tucking it inside, folding the corners as for the ends, and stapling it in place.

Screw castors onto the four corners, fill up the ottoman and put on the lid!

15

CD storage

Bought CD storage units never seem to fit in with other furnishings, but this neat tower holds well over a hundred CDs and has different coloured planes to co-ordinate with your décor.

CDs, like LPs, are difficult to store: piles topple over and end up spread all over the floor. Most bought CD storage seems to be black or pine – not very inspiring to look at and sometimes difficult to blend with existing room decoration.

You can plan the exact measurements to suit the size of tower you require. The one shown here holds an amazing 120 CDs neatly displayed on shelves. Made from versatile MDF, it has legs at the front and castors at the back to make it easy to move about.

The idea behind this design was to make the tower look more like a piece of furniture rather than simply a storage unit. It is painted in a combination of three colours, each side different, and you can choose whatever will match or complement your own room setting. The castors allow you to turn the tower so that only the coloured side can be seen, when it becomes more of a display stand for perhaps a small sculpture or a vase of flowers.

This design could also be adapted to make a tower for paperback books. Again, careful planning and measuring at the outset will ensure you make a unit that is attractive as well as functional.

Planning your time

DAY ONE
AM: Buy your materials. Cut out the pieces. Paint the inside pieces in your chosen colour.

PM: Position the shelves. Drill holes for the legs.
Put the top, bottom and sides together.

DAY TWO
AM: Make and fix the legs and castors. Prime.

PM: Apply two coats of colour.

Tools and materials

A sheet of 15 mm (½ in) MDF

Jigsaw

Primer

3 different colours of top coat

Panel pins

Hammer

Countersinking tool (pilot hole drill bit)

PVA glue

2 castors

2 offcuts of softwood

Plane

Sandpaper

Filler

Softwood batten as width gauge

1

2

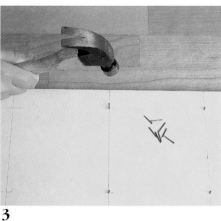

3

4

5

Day One

Step 1

Cut the MDF pieces to size (or ask your DIY store to do it for you). Using primer followed by two or three top coats in your chosen colour, paint inside the sides and back. Leave to dry between coats. To mark the position of the shelves on the inside of the side pieces, start measuring 15 mm (½ in) from the top (to allow for the top), and draw a line every 15 cm (6 in). Leave 15 mm (½ in) for the base.

Step 2

Using a long piece of softwood as a width gauge, mark the positions for two panel pins on each of the lines drawn for the shelves. Repeat on the inside of the opposite side so that each pair of pins will align.

Step 3

Hammer in the panel pins where you have marked their positions. Drive them in about halfway so that they can support the shelves adequately.

Step 4

Drill two countersunk holes (for the legs) in the front corners of the base.

Step 5

Join the back and one side together, by gluing and countersinking screws through the back and side.

Step 6

Join the top, base and second side.

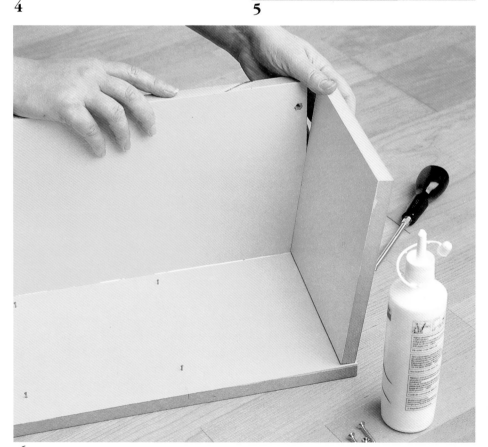

6

Day Two

Step 7

The two front legs should be the same height as the castors that go on the back. So cut two square blocks of wood the height of the castors (offcuts will do). Mark them up as shown in the photograph so that they taper at the front. Plane away the excess wood and sand the legs smooth.

Step 8

Turn the CD tower upside down, and screw the castors into the back of the base. Place the legs at the front and mark them through the holes that you drilled in the base in step 4.

Step 9

Drill a pilot hole in the centre of each leg, position the legs and screw them on through the drilled hole in the base.

Step 10

Fill all the holes and joins with all-purpose filler; you may need to do this several times as the filler shrinks as it dries. Sand down when dry each time.

Step 11

Apply primer paint to the outside and the shelves. When dry, rub down lightly and apply two or three coats of main colour. When thoroughly dry, slot in the shelves on top of the pairs of panel pins and load up with CDs. If the shelves are rather too snug, sand the sides until they fit easily.

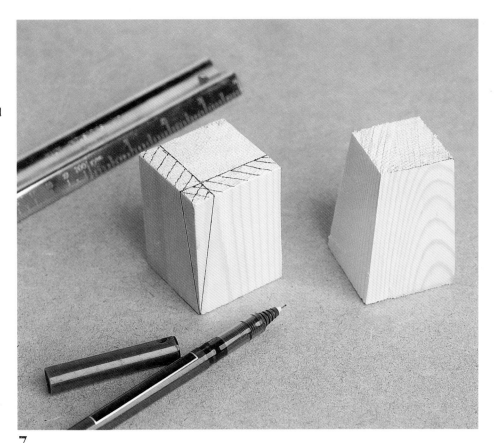

7

8

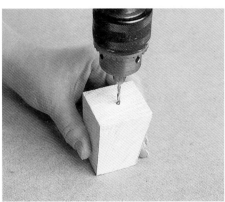

9

10

11

MDF shaped screen with blind

This is a great idea for making full use of an alcove that is too big for a single wardrobe and too small for a double. The idea is simple, but looks most effective.

Planning your time

DAY ONE
AM: Buy your materials.
Fix battens to walls.

PM: Cut out the MDF and fit to battens. Prime.

DAY TWO
AM: Apply two to three coats of top colour.

PM: Fix blind.

Tools and materials

A sheet of 15 mm (½ in) MDF,
1.2 x 2.4 m (4 x 8 ft)
(get this cut down to 1.8 m [6 ft]
when you buy it)

Softwood battens

Screws and wall plugs

Spirit level

PVA glue

Felt pen

Jigsaw

Hammer

Panel pins

Nail punch

Filler and fine sandpaper

Primer paint

Top colour paint

Roller blind to fit

lcoves are usually either shelved or have hanging rails in them, neither of which look particularly attractive. They are difficult to keep tidy, mainly because not everything you own is the same shape and size, so refuses to fit neatly together. The best solution is to hide everything.

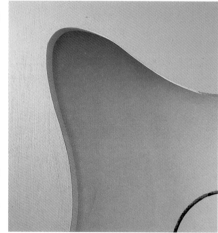

You can make this screen for an alcove less than 1.2 m (4 ft) wide with one sheet of MDF; if it is any wider you will have to join two pieces. Draw a random shape on a sheet of MDF, making sure you do not have too many thin bits or the MDF might split or break when you cut it. Use a jigsaw to cut it out and get someone to support the centre piece as you do so. Cutting out this amount may take some time, so be patient.

The blind is a shop-bought roller blind, with a design drawn on with a felt marker pen. I just drew around three different-sized plates to make the curved shapes, but you could try tracing simple shapes from enlarged photocopies if you are not confident about drawing freehand. You could also cut out pictures and glue them along the bottom edge.

Day One

Step 1

Measure the height and width of the alcove. The alcove shown here is 1.2 m (4 ft) wide, the width of a sheet of MDF. If your alcove is wider you will need to join two sheets of MDF.

Mark the height of the screen on the back wall and screw on a softwood batten, cut to length. Make pilot holes first in the wood and in the wall; use wall plugs for the screws to grip into. Use a spirit level to make sure the batten is straight.

Step 2

Cut two more softwood battens the depth of the alcove, minus the width of the MDF and back batten, so that the screen will be flush to the wall when fitted. Screw these in to the left and right of the back batten. Again, use a spirit level to get them straight. These battens will support the top shelf.

Step 3

Place battens vertically down the two side walls, using a spirit level to get them straight, keeping them in line with the top shelf.

Step 4

Nail battens into the floor, on either side of the screen, to support the bottom edges, preventing them moving.

Step 5

Fix the mechanism for the blind to the underside of the shelf. Do this before you fix the screen.

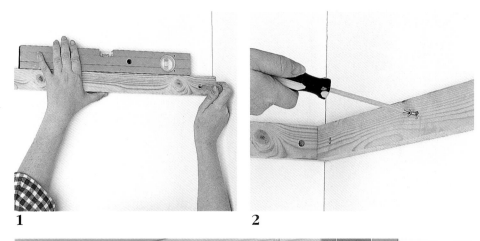

1

2

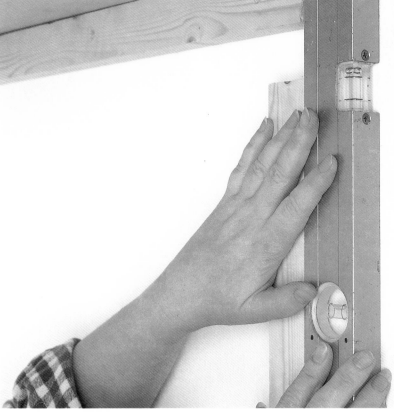

3

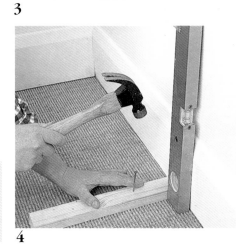

4

5

Safety note

Always wear a mask when cutting MDF.

Step 6

Draw the shape of the screen on a sheet of MDF with a thick-nibbed felt pen. Do not make any part of the shape too narrow or you will have difficulty cutting it out. Remember to make the bottom edges as long as the softwood floor battens.

Cut out the shape with a jigsaw. You will need to support the screen on trestles as you cut. Have a helper on hand to take the weight of the middle section as you cut it out.

Step 7

Make a template of the skirting and transfer it to the floor edge of the MDF screen and cut it out. Reverse the image for the opposite side. You might need to sand the shape down slightly if it does not fit accurately.

Step 8

Apply PVA glue to the batten edges and the edge of the top shelf.

Step 9

Nail the screen to the battens and hit them home with a nail punch. This will leave small indentations in the wood, so fill these small holes with all-purpose filler and, when dry, sand down. Paint on a coat of primer.

Day Two

Step 10

When the primer is dry paint two or three coats of top colour. When dry, hang the blind. I drew around different-sized plates with a felt pen, but you can decorate it as you please, or choose a plain blind that matches your décor.

6

7

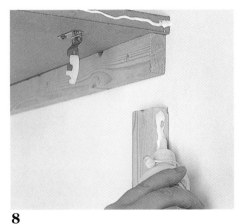

8

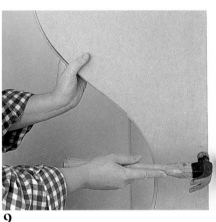

9

10

Making and covering boxes

Boxes are easy to make and you can design them for specific items such as photographs or stationery. Cover them with remnants to match your existing furnishings.

Planning your time

DAY ONE
AM: Buy your materials. Work out the sizes for the boxes.

PM: Make the base and lid for the circular box. Cover with fabric.

DAY TWO
AM: Make the base and lid for the rectangular box.

PM: Cover with fabric. Attach the name plate.

Tools and materials

Mount board

Calculator

Metal ruler

Ticket card

Gummed paper

PVA glue

Enough fabric to cover the finished boxes

Scissors

Masking tape

Cutting mat

Craft knife

Bradawl

Name plate

String

Why make your own boxes?' you might ask, when there are plenty of discarded boxes available for your storage needs. Well, if you design and make them yourself you will have boxes that are exactly the size you want for a specific storage job. For instance, the round box here was made to hold small cosmetics bottles, which are usually difficult to store upright. You can design series of boxes for items you want to store, and they will all fit neatly into that awkwardly shaped cupboard.

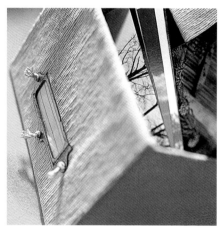

Boxes custom built to hold particular items or objects can be further designed for more specific uses – for example, by making your own dividers to catalogue photos by subject or date, or to categorize computer disks in a home office. Children will love lots of tiny square compartments to keep small 'treasures' safe and separate.

This idea is perfect for using up smaller fabric remnants that would otherwise be folded up in a drawer or simply thrown away. Covered in co-ordinating material, these boxes will be attractive accessories in any room.

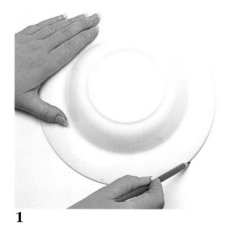

1

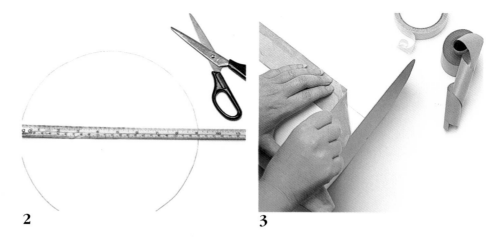

3

2

Day One

Step 1

To make a round box, draw around a plate or use a compass to draw a circle for the size of base you want. Draw it on a sheet of stiff card (mount board is best) or the base will buckle and cut it out with scissors.

Step 2

To work out the circumference of the circle, measure the diameter and multiply the figure by pi (3.142). This gives you the width of the piece of card you need to cut for the sides. Cut a sheet of ticket card 30 cm (12 in) high (or whatever size you want) by the figure you have just calculated.

Step 3

Roll the ticket card into a tube, butting the two edges together, and holding it in place with masking tape. Wet a strip of gummed paper and place it over the join. Fold the excess down the join inside the tube.

Step 4

Push the base down through the tube, until it is about 1 mm (¹⁄₁₆ in) from the bottom. You might need a few attempts at this!

4

Cutting a circle of fabric

If you have trouble making the fabric fit a circle, snip it at 1 cm (½ in) intervals and cut out small 'V's so that it lies flat.

Step 5

Secure the base of the box in place with a line of PVA glue around the join. It will make quite a strong bond when the glue has dried.

Step 6

Cut a piece of fabric to cover the outside of the box and add on 4 cm (1½ in) to the width and depth. I chose a ribbed fabric that has an interesting selvedge so that I did not have to turn under a hem. Glue the material onto the outside, overlapping the join, turn over 2 cm (¾ in) of fabric into the inside of the box and glue in place. Turn the box upside down and snip around the edge of the fabric and glue in place, overlapping the snips to make a neat edge.

Step 7

Cut out a circle of fabric (draw round the plate or use a compass again) and glue onto the base.

Step 8

The lid needs to be 1 cm (½ in) bigger than its box to accommodate two thicknesses of fabric. Draw around the same plate (or use the compass set at 5 mm [¼ in] bigger than the base) with an italic-nib marker on its thickest side.

Make the lid in the same way as the base. Obviously the rim will only be about 6 cm (2½ in) deep, but make it in proportion to the box. To cover the lid, cut the circle of cloth bigger, glue it onto the lid, snip the excess and glue down onto the outside of the rim. Cut a strip of fabric to fit the rim with a 2 cm (¾ in) hem, glue in place and glue the excess fabric onto the inside.

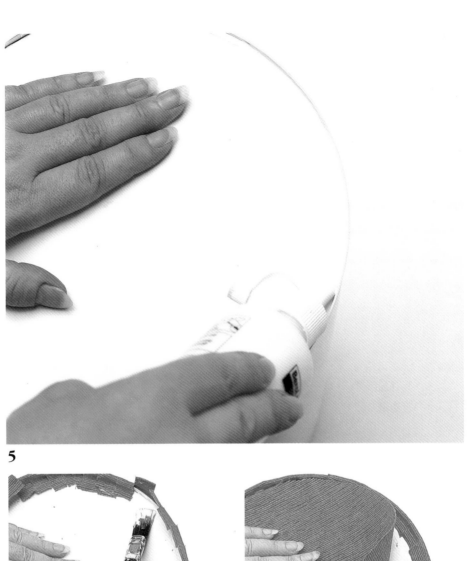

5

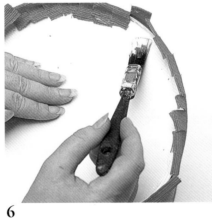

6

7

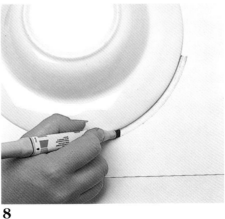

8

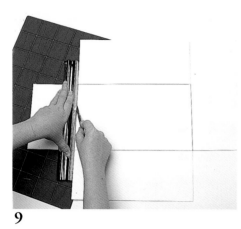

9

10

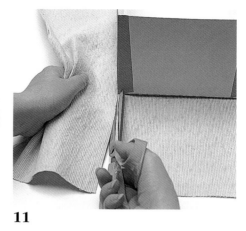

11

Day Two

Step 9

I made this rectangular box 13 cm (5¼ in) high x 18.5 cm (7¼ in) wide x 30 cm (12 in) long to hold photographs. Measure out the base on a piece of mount board (30 x 18.5 cm [12 x 7¼ in]) and measure the sides as shown. Cut out the flat shape of the box with a craft knife on a cutting board. Then score along the pencil lines, but do not cut right through.

Step 10

Turn the card over and fold the box along the scored lines and join each side with gummed paper.

Step 11

Cut a piece of fabric to fit the box with a 2 cm (¾ in) overlap on each side. Place the base in the middle of the fabric piece and glue in place. Cut the fabric along the grain so that it will fit the front and end of the box.

Step 12

Glue the longer sides in place first with 1 cm (½ in) overlap and trim off the excess fabric.

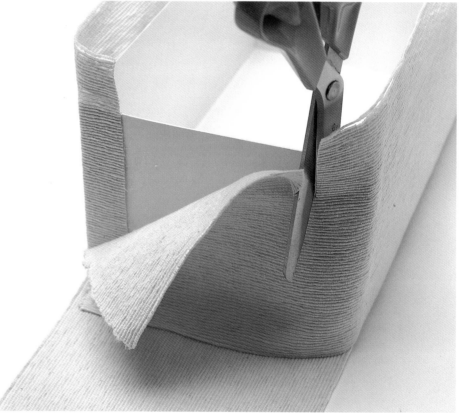

12

Choosing card

When making the lid and base of a box, particularly a round one, it is important to use a reasonably stiff card; a thin card will buckle. Mount board is recommended, because although it is stiff you can still cut it with scissors.

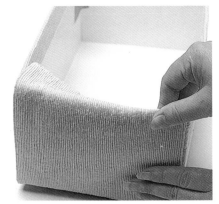

13

14

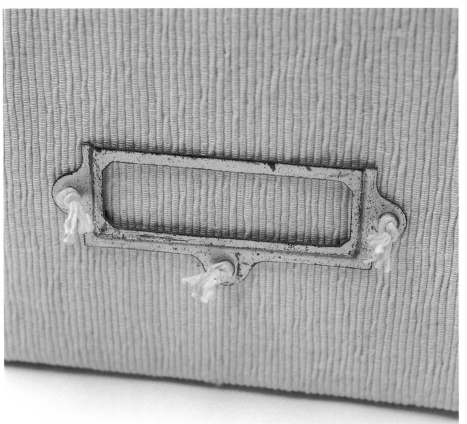

15

Step 13
Glue the front and end in place and turn the excess fabric into the inside and glue in place.

Step 14
To attach the name plate to the front of the box, mark its position by puncturing three holes with a bradawl through the screw holes.

Step 15
Cut three small pieces of string and knot them all at one end. Line up the name plate and push the pieces of string through the holes. Secure on the other side with another knot or masking tape.

Step 16
Make the lid in proportion to the box in the same way as the lid for the round box (Step 8), making it 1 cm (½ in) larger all round, to take the fabric thickness.

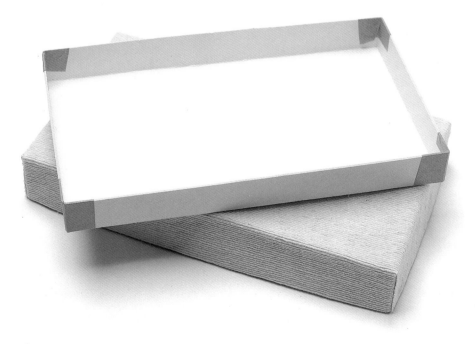

16

Underbed shoe platform

This storage platform keeps everyday shoes to hand, makes use of redundant space and requires no effort to use – three good reasons for taking the time to put it together.

I love this idea, as it makes use of space under a bed that would otherwise be wasted. It solves the problem of where to keep shoes, especially if you have lots of pairs; I do not find shoe boxes easy to use and never seem to put them back in their proper place.

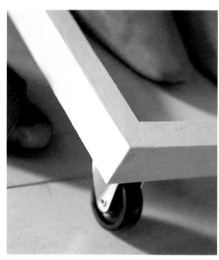

You can fit two of these platforms under a double bed – his and hers! Making the shoe platform will probably only take you a day, apart from the painting, thus leaving you time for other weekend activities. I bought a 61 x 92 cm (2 x 3 ft) sheet of MDF and had the battening cut to fit the edges when I bought it. All you really do then is glue the pieces together and paint the assembled platform. Castors allow you to move the platform in and out from under the bed in an instant.

An underbed platform can provide useful storage for other items, depending on the depth of space available. Even the narrowest of spaces could probably be useful for storing magazines or linen.

Planning your time

DAY ONE
AM: Buy your materials. Cut the battening and glue in place.

PM: Fill joints, fix castors and prime. Apply first coat of top colour.

DAY TWO
AM: Sand lightly, apply second coat, leave to dry.

PM: Apply third coat or varnish if necessary.

Tools and materials

A pre-cut sheet of 12 mm (⅜ in) thick MDF,
60 x 90 cm (2 x 3 ft)

20 x 25 mm (¾ x 1 in) softwood for the edges

PVA glue

Filler and filling knife

Fine sandpaper

4 castors on fixing plates

Bradawl

Fine drill bit

All-purpose primer

Eggshell top coat in your chosen colour

Day One

Step 1

I bought a pre-cut sheet of 12 mm
(½ in) thick MDF measuring 60 x 90 cm
(2 x 3 ft). I also had the softwood
battening cut to fit around the four
edges at the shop, remembering to
deduct twice its width from the shorter
pieces. Apply PVA glue to all four pieces
along the corresponding edges.

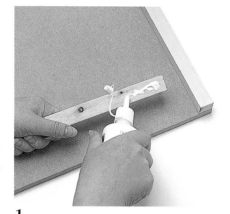

1

2

Step 2

Butt the joints together. Wipe off any
excess glue that squeezes out from the
sides and hold the battens in place
until the glue is tacky. Turn the platform
over and put some heavy objects
around the edge to weight it down
until the glue sets.

Step 3

Turn the platform back on its right side
and fill all the joints and knot holes
with all-purpose filler, then rub down
with fine sandpaper around a cork
sanding block.

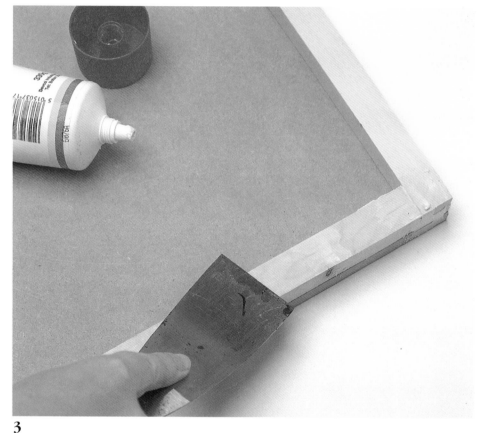

3

Step 4

On the underneath, mark the position
of the castors by putting a pencil mark
through the screw holes. Position the
castors as near to the edge as possible,
without being right on the edge, so
that the screws will screw through
both the thickness of the MDF and
the pine battens. Make pilot holes with
a bradawl first to prevent the MDF
from splitting.

Step 5

Drill pilot holes for the three corners of
the castor that are over the softwood
battening. Use a drill bit that is a size
smaller than the screws so that the
thread grips the MDF.

4

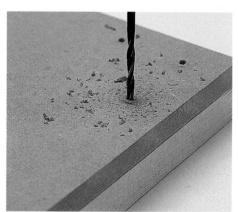

5

6

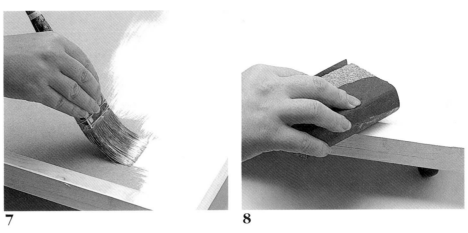

7

8

Step 6

Screw the castors into the three corners over the softwood battening, turning the castor to reach each screw position. Putting the castors on first will keep the platform off the floor while you are painting it.

Step 7

Apply an oil-based primer paint if you are going to use eggshell paint or water-based primer for emulsion paint. I did not paint the underside, but if you want to, it is easier to do this before you put on the castors.

Step 8

Rub down lightly after priming and between each subsequent coat of paint. Use a fine grade sandpaper or 'wet and dry' paper over a cork sanding block; a block makes sanding flat surfaces much easier. Apply a coat of eggshell paint and leave to dry.

Day Two

Step 9

Apply one or two coats of eggshell paint, sanding between coats. Eggshell and gloss paint are more hardwearing than emulsion, but if you use a water-based paint apply two coats of varnish to protect the platform. When thoroughly dry fill the plaform up with shoes and wheel it under the bed.

9

Pull-up curtains for freestanding shelving

These pull-up curtains make a neat way to disguise untidy shelves, especially if the room has a dual purpose – where a dining room doubles as a sewing room, for instance.

We rarely seem to have enough space to dedicate one room to a hobby or favourite pastime, and in small, modern homes some rooms have to serve several purposes.

Dining rooms are seldom used just for eating, so the concept behind this project is to help make the best of the shelving and space you may already have in a room that has to double as an office, or as a space to pursue hobbies. If you have to tidy away at the end of the day you can hide your work behind these pull-up curtains.

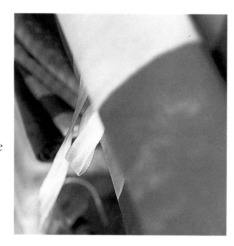

This idea would work just as well for computer equipment, china or children's toys, but if you do use these curtains with children about, make sure you secure the shelving to the wall first.

The hook and loop fastener makes the curtains easy to remove for washing or you could make different curtains for different occasions, or swap them around according to the time of year. The curtains could even become one of the main decorative features in the room.

Day One

Step 1

Assemble the shelving. Measure the width at the front and attach the sticky side of the hook and loop fastener.

Step 2

Using pinking shears, cut the fabric to fit the front, adding on 2 cm (¾ in) to the top, bottom and each side for the hems. Centre any pattern over the front of the shelving.

Turn under a 2 cm (¾ in) hem all round and machine in place, except for the top.

Step 3

Cut two lengths of webbing the length of the fabric, adding on 2 cm (¾ in). Pin it 10 cm (4 in) in from each edge and turn 2 cm (¾ in) onto the reverse side at the top.

Step 4

Pin the sew part of the hook and loop fastener to the reverse side of the top edge – over the webbing – and machine stitch in place.

Day Two

Step 5

Mark positions for the eyelets with a pencil, along the line that the webbing hangs. Position these at 10 cm (4 in) intervals down the length of the fabric, or as here, on the edge of each square. Make sure that, when it is threaded, the last eyelet will bring the webbing to hang on the front of the fabric, not behind.

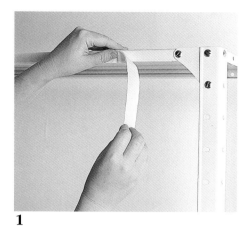

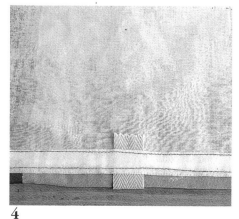

1

2

3

4

5

Step 6

Hammer in an eyelet on each mark. Thread the webbing through the eyelets. Repeat on the other side of the curtain.

Step 7

Turn the curtain over and sew on a casing, leaving the ends open, 10 cm (4 in) up from the lower edge. Cut a piece of half-round dowelling, slightly narrower than the curtain, and slot it inside the casing.

Step 8

When the curtain is raised it is held in place with a loose knot. The dowelling will keep the bottom line straight.

Step 9

The side curtains do not need to pull up and down, so the top and sides of the fabric need to be edged with hook and loop fastener. Cut the fabric to fit the sides, adding on 2 cm (¾ in). Press a 2 cm (¾ in) hem onto the wrong side, pin the sew part of the hook and loop fastener onto the top and sides. Sew in place, taking the stitching along the bottom edge to sew the hem.

Step 10

Fix the sticky hook and loop fastener to the sides of the shelves. Attach the curtains to the shelves. Use this method to make as many curtains as you need!

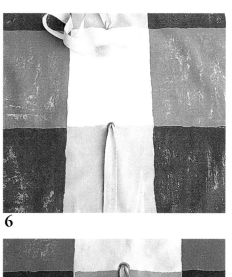

6

7

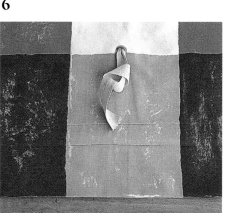

8

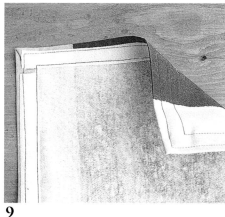

9

10

Hanging pocket tidy

Here is a go-anywhere solution to those small items that you need at hand, whether in a bathroom, kitchen or child's room. A pocket tidy will fit on the back of any door.

Pocket tidies used to be much more in use than they are now, but we have somehow forgotten about the idea. A tidy is the perfect place for all those little things that you have to have but do not know what to do with.

There is no reason why you cannot make the tidy to any size. I made this one to fit on the back of a door, but you could make one to go inside a cupboard, or on a spare area of wall. Do not make the pockets too big or they will fall forward when you fill them. You could stiffen them with Vilene on the inside of the pocket strip before you sew it to the edges.

Use a co-ordinating fabric to match your other furnishings, or make the tidy from a large remnant. Another alternative is to use PVC, especially if you intend to use the pocket tidy in the kitchen or bathroom.

The tidy is, of course, transportable – ideal for taking on camping and caravanning holidays – and a slightly smaller version would easily roll up for packing in a suitcase.

Planning your time

DAY ONE

AM: Buy your materials, cut out the back and the pockets. Press and hem the sides and tops of the pockets.

PM: Sew the pockets and ribbon in place. Fold the pockets and sew ribbon in place.

DAY TWO

AM: Hammer in the eyelets and hang tidy on the wall.

PM: Go out for lunch and have a good time!

Tools and materials

Fabric, about 160 cm (1¾ yd) depending on required size of tidy

Thread

Sewing machine

Grosgrain ribbon

Pins

2 eyelets

Hammer

Half-round beading

2 hooks for hanging on the wall or door

Day One

Step 1

Cut a piece of fabric measuring 100 x 60 cm (40 x 24 in) for the back of the tidy. At the same time cut three strips for the pockets, each 90 cm (36 in) wide and 20 cm (8 in) deep. Press a 15 mm (½ in) hem on the sides of the back, onto the right side of the fabric.

Step 2

Turn under a 15 mm (½ in) hem on the top of the pocket strips, onto the wrong side of the fabric. Sew the hem on the pocket strips.

Step 3

Pin the pocket strips to the back, tucking the edges under the side hems. Pin one strip at the bottom edge; the next, 10 cm (4 in) from the top edge of the bottom strip; and the third, 10 cm (4 in) from the top edge of the middle pocket.

Step 4

Machine sew the strips in place.

Step 5

Cut four 100 cm (40 in) pieces of grosgrain ribbon. Sew two of the pieces onto the outside edges of the back, to cover the hem and edges of the pockets. Place the other two evenly within the width of the back, so that there are three pockets. The fabric should be loose from side to side.

1

2

3

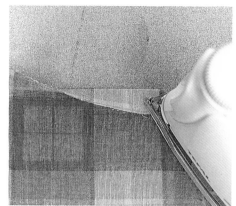

4

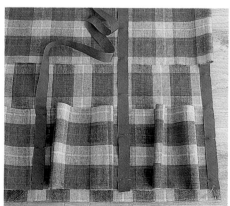

5

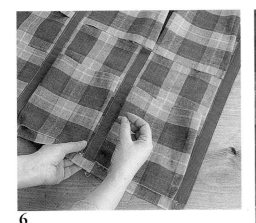

6

Step 6

Fold the pockets so that they have a
pleat in each side, but sit within the
ribbon. Pin in place.

Step 7

Press a 15 mm (½ in) hem at the top
and bottom of the tidy onto the right
side of the fabric.

Step 8

Cut four pieces of ribbon to fit the
width of the tidy, adding 2 cm (1 in) to
tuck under at the sides. Pin them across
the top edge of the tidy and bottom
edges of the pockets and sew in place.

Day Two

Step 9

Make a hole in the top two corners and
hammer in eyelets.

Step 10

Turn the pocket tidy over and sew a
casing above the line of the top pocket,
leaving the ends open – you can use an
offcut of ribbon for this. Cut a piece of
half-round beading slightly shorter than
the casing and slot inside. Attach two
hooks to the door and hang up the tidy.

7

8

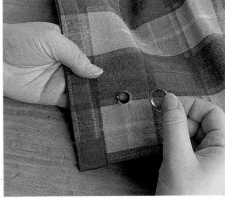

9

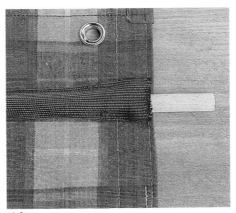

10

Freestanding folding screen

A screen like this can hide a pile of clutter, instantly solving your storage problems as it needs no fixed position. It also serves to divide rooms and makes an attractive focal point.

A padded screen is more like a piece of furniture than a functional object, but it is a simple way to hide things that you just do not know what to do with or that you have not had time to put away when visitors call. The padding gives it softness and means that the screen can also double as a pinboard to keep notes or postcards on display.

The panels consist of softwood frames with plywood pinned to them, which you can get cut to size at the shop. Covered in wadding and fabric, it can be treated as a piece of upholstery and you can choose fabric to match curtains or other pieces of furniture you might have in the room.

Old Victorian screens are much in demand now, but many require a great deal of restoration work and re-covering to make them presentable. The screen shown here could be made up in a period fabric at a fraction of the cost, giving you a versatile and fashionable piece of furniture. It is light to handle and castors make it easy to wheel around to different rooms in the home as the need arises.

Planning your time

DAY ONE
AM: Work out the size of the panels and buy all your materials. Get the wood cut to size at the DIY store if you can.

PM: Make the three panels from the plywood and softwood battening.

DAY TWO
AM: Cover the panels with wadding, fabric and ribbon.

PM: Screw in the castors, join the panels together with hinges, and put in place.

Tools and materials

6 sheets of 4 mm (⅛ in) plywood, 60 cm x 2.5 m (2 x 8 ft) cut to 60 cm x 1.8 m (2 x 6ft)

25 x 33 mm (1 x 1¼ in) softwood battening to make the frames

PVA glue

Panel pins

Wadding

Staple gun and staples

Fabric to cover the screen

Grosgrain ribbon to fit around the edge of all three panels

6 castors, 12 mm (½ in) drill bit (or appropriate size for castors)

Six strong hinges

Day One

Step 1

For three panels, I bought six sheets of 4 mm (⅙ in) plywood measuring 60 cm x 2.5 m (2 x 8 ft) and had them cut down to 1.8 m (6 ft) in the shop.

Cut lengths of 25 x 33 mm (1 x 1¼ in) softwood to fit along the edges of three of the plywood sheets. Lay the battens on the floor and glue them on the 25 mm (1 in) edge.

Step 2

Lay the plywood on top of the glued frame, making sure the edges match up.

Step 3

To make one panel, pin the plywood to the frame with panel pins.

1

2

3

Fixing hinges to a screen

There is a great deal of stress on the joins of a folding screen, so it is important to have strong hinges, as they will take a lot of wear and tear. Ideally you should have at least three to five hinges, spaced evenly over the length of each join. The fixing plates should be just as wide as the thickness of the panel, with three screw holes in each side.

4

5

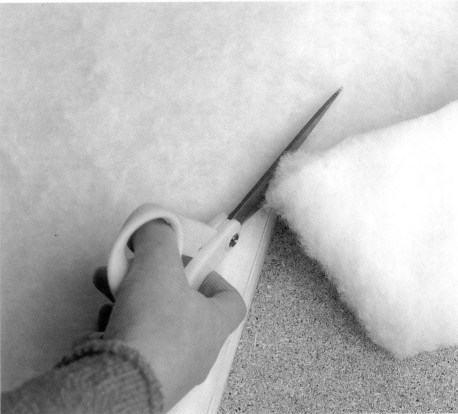

6

Step 4
Cut two blocks from the leftover softwood, and glue and nail them to the bottom inside corners of the panels. These are to screw the castors into later.

Step 5
Mark the bottom edge on the outside of the frame. Glue and pin a second sheet of plywood onto the other side. Make the other two panels like this.

Day Two

Step 6
Lay the panel on the floor and cut the wadding to size widthways and a little shorter lengthways, as it may stretch.

Step 7
Staple the wadding to both sides of the panel with a staple gun.

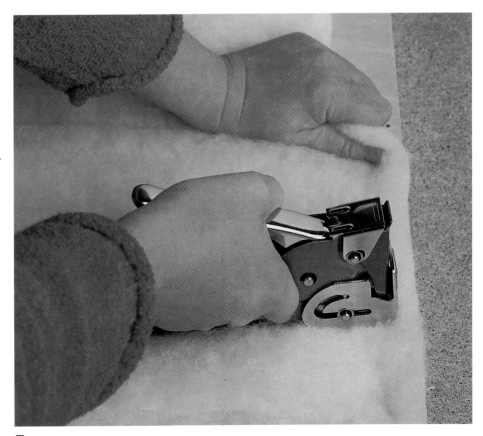

7

8

10

9

Step 8

Cover one side of the panel with fabric.
I chose a check, and a stripe for the
reverse from the same fabric collection.
Staple the fabric along the top edge,
then pull it taut while stapling the
bottom edge. Do not pull it too tight or
the pattern may become distorted.

Step 9

Staple the sides. Then fold the corners
as shown in the photograph and staple
in place, so that the top of the fold lies
along the edge of the frame.

Step 10

Before you staple the fabric to the
other side, mark the bottom edge with
a piece of paper pinned to the fabric,
or a sticky label.

Step 11

Staple fabric to the reverse side of the
panel. Staple as near to the centre as
you can and trim off any excess fabric.

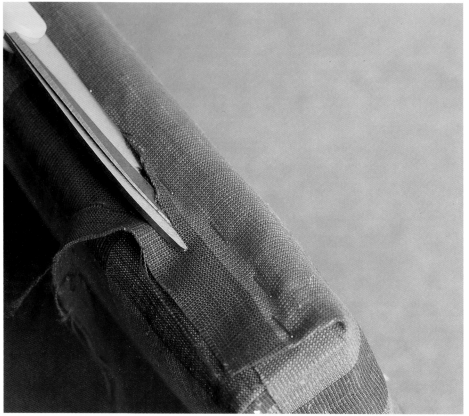

11

Step 12

Glue grosgrain ribbon all along the edges of the frame to cover the staples. Join the ribbon on the bottom edge.

Step 13

Drill a hole 4 cm (1½ in) in from each corner on the bottom edge using a 12 mm (½ in) drill bit. Hammer in the casing for the castor.

Step 14

Push the castor up into the casing. Repeat on the other side of the panel.

Step 15

Join the panels together in a concertina fashion with three strong hinges on each join.

12

13

14

15

Glossary

Flat wood drill bit

Bradawl

Mitre block

Beading
Ready-made strips of wood, sometimes ornate, or half or quarter-round for decoration on furniture or walls.

Bradawl
A tool used to make a small hole in wood before fixing panel pins or screws – the starter hole helps prevent the wood from splitting.

Countersinking screws
When a screw lies below the surface of the wood it is 'countersunk'. You can buy countersunk screws with flat tops for this purpose.

Dowelling
A length of round wood with a small diameter that can easily be cut to whatever length required.

Filler
Ideal for filling holes, you can buy this in sachets and then add to water to make a paste, or buy ready-to-use filler in a tube or tub.

Flat wood drill bit
A flat blade-like drill attachment with a pointed end for drilling large holes in wood. The point is used to make a pilot hole for the flat blade.

Florists' wire
Soft, pliable wire used by florists in flower arranging. It is very similar to fuse wire.

Gummed paper
Available from art shops, gummed paper comes on a roll. The gum is on one side of the paper and needs wetting to make it sticky.

Jigsaw
An electric saw that allows you to cut intricate shapes. It has a base plate that can be angled for cutting. Different grades of blade give a different quality of cut.

Joining (mending) plates
Rectangular pieces of metal used to join wood in a 'T' join or mend wood if it has split.

Key
A key is a rough surface to which paint can adhere, prepared by rubbing down with sandpaper or wire wool.

Knotting
A colourless liquid used to seal the knots in wood. Knots will ooze resin if not treated, which will discolour paint and form bubbles on the surface. Pine is a particularly knotty wood.

Medium density fibreboard (MDF)
MDF is made from particles of wood and dust that are bonded together under very high pressure. It makes an ideal surface for painting as there is no grain and you can achieve a good flat finish. It is available in sheets of various

sizes. When cutting MDF you should always wear a mask as a protection against the high dust content.

Mitre

A mitre is a 45-degree angle cut. The easiest way to cut a mitre is to use a mitre box and tenon saw.

Mitre box (or block)

A block designed to help cut diagonal angles for corners (from wood or plaster) so that the butted pieces make a 45-degree angle. It has a ready-cut slot to guide your saw.

Mount board

Mount board is a card that is used as a mount for pictures and photographs. It is available in a wide range of colours and textures from art shops and framing suppliers.

Nail punch

A metal tool that enables you to knock the head of a nail below the surface of the wood. Its hollow-ground tapered tip is the diameter of a panel pin or small nail, and its top is flat so that it can be hit with a hammer.

Paint (emulsion)

A water-based paint that is easy to use and can be applied with a paintbrush or roller. It is available in both matt and silk finishes. It is fast drying, so you need to work quickly with it.

Paint (oil-based)

This paint is available in gloss, eggshell and flat finishes and produces a durable and waterproof coating. It should be applied in layers, beginning with a primer and undercoat. Oil-based paints take longer to dry; large items should be left overnight to dry completely.

Pilot hole drill bit (countersink tool)

A drill piece that allows you to drill a pilot hole into two pieces of wood that are to be screwed together. The drill countersinks the screw head at the same time.

Plane

A plane is a tool that allows you to shave or smooth wood accurately and finely.

Priming

New or stripped wood should always be given a coat of primer before any other type of paint is applied to it. Look out for primers and undercoats that are combined, as these will save valuable time. Previously painted wood does not need a primer, but sand down old paint to provide a good key for the undercoat.

PVA glue

A white water-based glue that gives a strong bond. Watered down, it can be used as a sealant. When dry, it loses its milky look and gives a clear finish.

Round-nosed pliers

Nail punch

Staple gun

Wall plugs

Wirecutters

Wing bolt

Round-nosed pliers
Bends wire without flattening it.

Sanding block
Sandpaper wrapped around a wood or cork block.

Softwood batten
Strips of wood, usually cheaper cuts, used to make frames to which other materials are attached. A common example of a softwood is pine.

Spirit level
Enables you to get lines straight. When the bubble is in the centre of the level, the surface it is on is straight.

Stanley knife
A heavy craft knife with sharp, disposable, and sometimes retractable, blades.

Staple gun
Used for attaching fabric to wood, or softwood frames.

Tenon saw
A short fine-toothed saw for cutting joints in wood.

Velcro
The trade name for hook and loop fastener. The Sew 'n' Stick version is used for a number of projects in this book. One side of the fastener is sewn to fabric, the other is stuck to a substrate.

Vice
A vice will hold a piece of wood in place while you work on it. Usually a vice is screwed onto a workbench in a workshop, but portable work benches, such as a Workmate, also have an integral vice.

Wadding
Available in various thicknesses (or weights). Polyester wadding is fully washable.

Wall plugs
Enable you to screw into a wall or plasterboard where there is no natural grip for the thread of the screw. Wall plugs expand as the screw is turned. You should select the right size plug for the screws you are using.

Wing bolt
A wing bolt opens out to grip the substrate when its screw end is tightened.

Wirecutters
For cutting wire. A good pair of combination pliers will also do the job.

Wire wool
Very fine strands of wire intertwined to look like a hank of wool. This can be used for rubbing down shiny surfaces to give a key for painting or for buffing up.

Suppliers

Anna French
343 King's Road, London SW3 5ES
(Tel. 0171 351 1126)
*Fabric in curtain-covered alcove
project, page 8*

Art In Iron
Unit F, Bridges Wharf, Bridges Court,
off York Road, London SW11 3AD
(Tel. 0171 924 2332)
*Bed and mattress in underbed shoe
platform project, page 58 and making
and covering boxes project, page 52*

Crown Paints
PO Box 37, Crown House, Hollins Road,
Darwen, Lancashire BB3 0BG
(Tel. 01254 704951)
Paint used throughout

Crowson Fabrics
Crowson House, Bellbrook Park,
Uckfield, East Sussex TN22 1QZ
(Tel. 01825 761055)
*Fabric in freestanding folding screen
project, page 70*

David Mellor
4 Sloane Square, London SW1 8EE
(Tel. 0171 730 4259)
*Cookware in peg rail project, page 34
and wall ladder project, page 20*

George Petersen
152 Upper Street, London N1
(Tel. 0171 359 5655)
Dining table, chairs and glasses in

*pull-up curtains for freestanding
shelving project, page 62*

Johnson Bros,
Barlaston, Stoke on Trent ST12 9ES
(Tel. 017822 204141)
*Tableware in pull-up curtains for
freestanding shelving project, page 62*

Melin Tregwynt
Tregwynt Mill, Castle Morris,
Haverfordwest, Pembrokeshire,
Dyfed SA62 5UX
*Blankets in making and covering
boxes project, page 52 and pull-up
curtains for freestanding shelving
project, page 62*

Paperchase
213 Tottenham Court Road,
London W1P 9AF
(Tel. 0171 580 8496)
*Stationery and storage boxes in
hanging shelves on chains project,
page 30*

Threshold Flooring
Vorda Works, Highworth, Swindon, Wilts
(Tel. 01793 764301)
*Flooring in MDF shaped screen with
blind project, page 48, ottoman
project, page 38 and freestanding
folding screen project, page 70*

Turquaz
31–33 The South Bank Business Centre,
Ponton Road, London SW8 5BL

(Tel. 0171 501 4200)
*Bedlinen in making and covering
boxes project, page 52 and underbed
shoe platform project, page 58*

Viners
106 Brent Terrace, London NW2 1BZ
(Tel. 0181 450 8900)
*Cutlery in pull-up curtains for
freestanding shelving project, page 62
and saucepans in wall ladder project,
page 20*

Wesley Barrell
Park Street, Charlbury, Oxford OX7 3PT
(Tel. 01608 810481)
*Armchair in freestanding folding
screen project, page 70*

Whitehead Fabrics
Dominion Way West, Southdownview
Road, Worthing, West Sussex BN14 8NW
(Tel. 01903 212222)
*Fabric in transforming a Formica
wardrobe project, page 24 and pull-up
curtains for freestanding shelving
project, page 62*

Wicanders
Amorim House, Star Road, Partridge
Green, Horsham, West Sussex RH13 8RA
(Tel. 01403 710001)
*Flooring in pull-up curtains for
freestanding shelving project, page 62
and transforming a Formica
wardrobe project, page 24*

Index